The Children of Separation

BRIAN JONES

The Children of Separation

Carcanet

ACKNOWLEDGEMENTS

Acknowledgements are made to *The London Magazine*, *Poems for Shakespeare* and *P.N. Review*.

First published in 1985 by
Carcanet Press Ltd
208-212 Corn Exchange Buildings
Manchester M4 3BQ

British Library Cataloguing in Publication Data

Jones, Brian, *1938-*
The Children of Separation
I. Title
821′.914 PR6060.049

ISBN 0-85635-620-4

The Publisher acknowledges financial assistance
from the Arts Council of Great Britain

Typeset by Bryan Williamson, Swinton, Berwickshire
Printed in England by SRP Ltd., Exeter

for Noëlle

Contents

Introductory : 1944

1. *Fed and Watered*

Here is my generation. We are ranked in a hall
neat and crammed as sprigs in a seed-box.
Outside, the first harvest we have ever known
is steadily reaped with softly whirring blades
and rabbits squeal and leap through an air
whirled gold. We groan a withheld sensual
ecstasy, yearning to handle ourselves
and each other. And then we sing: *We plough*
the fields and scatter . . . In the aftermath
one of us walks forward and is caned,
the whistling downcurve slicing through the palm
which is severed but does not fall. All our hands
are guilty. Paired, we turn to each other,
fisted, clawed, our mouths wet with desire.

2. *The Attendants*

The June sun blazes, releasing richly from the garden shed
odours of creosote, dead geraniums and paraffin,
and from Mr Greville languorously sensual recall
of afternoons spent there with Mrs Evans, whose body
his hand explored as now it explores the curves and crevices
of his deadbeat sofa. Mrs Greville believes he labours
over a tract on tomatoes, a miracle crop of which
he produced in the summer of nineteen thirty six,
before there was war and evacuees.

He is the backbone of England, working at night to fashion
metal killing-objects in the factory near the canal,
on whose banks he munches sandwiches alone on moonlit
nights.
He passes watching homes on his ticking Rudge slow and stately

as the light departs, and they all say 'There goes Mr Greville',
drawing their curtains close, and settling down to hear Big Ben
chime,
comforted and unalert, writing no-news to relations,
while elsewhere rise bombers, searchlights and constellations.
At twelve, the London train beats past on time.

Mr Greville knows that life's logic is uneventfulness.
It is luck that throws up wondrous tomatoes, Mrs Evans,
and a trusting wife. Eat big and sleep deep. Do not interfere
with the world, and keep your eyes open for the pickings of
chance.
When he wakes in the afternoon he yawns and scratches his
crotch,
and on hearing the springs sigh, Mrs Greville prepares the toast.
He knows he is loved and trusted. His hand plunges more deeply
into the sofa as into opportunity.
Today, another war-flung woman comes.

Pauline will grow into a darkly mysterious woman.
Already she has fluttered several hearts among the beet-fields.
She has learned she has power, but has not yet exploited it,
has, instead, a dim mysterious sense of being exploited.
The London boys touched her body like musicians touching
strings,
and the music quivered in their cheeks. She did not feel music.
She has learned a thing or two for when another boy arrives.
Among the nettles by the station she keeps her eyes
staring southward. She will not miss a trick.

It is not easy to be teaching, to be alone, teaching,
in the uneventful Midlands, to pass your endless weekends
walking alone among the growing grain, feeling the skin teased,
feeling the prickle of sweat define the raw edge of yearning.
Miss Cowans hates the children with their futures and
whisperings,
the way heads sway in assembly conspiratorially,
the way the hands she canes are sticky with out-of-school horrors.

Faces stare back at her like impossible mirrors,
like the faces that face a refugee.

Peter is conspicuous for the sharpness of his dressing –
smart pale slacks, crisp shirts – and a look debonair and masterful.
But no-one understands his feelings, understands why he comes
every week to the station, to sit alone drawing the rails
narrowing into the distance their certainty of purpose.
He teaches the wounded in the transit camp, himself wounded
from birth by a withered ankle his fashionable slacks hide.
He knows that after the war there must be a new world.
Lonely students like himself will found it

who are now preparing themselves at night in cocoons of peace
as khaki heroes and demagogues hog bombarded stages
and loom large in the searchlights of simplicity. However,
he needs these weekly visits to where the railway lines run bright
southward to the heart of power, to cities that are waiting
for the arrival of peace, for men of knowledge and vision.
But the lines run two ways. He sits at the heart of arrival.
He yearns to give, but is an empty receptacle
awaiting love, the spur of social passion.

In nineteen eighty three, a train oddly anachronistic —
a lovely slow swayer with softly bouncing seats, corridors,
and windows set in walnut, so that the summer world passes
gradually and in incidents like so many paintings —
rocks towards the Midlands. On board, a man clutches a black
case
rich with unhappy poems which he will discharge that evening
guardedly to a scatter of listeners in Nottingham.
He is charmed into smile by this train, its old rhythms,
feeling a deep-set resistance yielding.

He will be lulled by this journey – as a child in mother's arms
drifts in a moving human warmth towards the abandonment
of grief – into a sleep he has not known since he was a child,
to awake stared at by a station and long level grainfields
and by a mother jauntily pretty in a pillbox hat,
who will shepherd him over the slatted wooden bridge towards
vast arrests of feeling, that will hold their shapes like armatures
and gather around themselves unfulfilling futures,
and foul all journeys but the journey backward.

Fancy Bread

an elegy

Tell me where is Fancy bred
Or in the heart or in the head?
How begot, how nourished?
        Reply, reply.
It is engendered in the eyes,
With gazing fed; and Fancy dies
In the cradle where it lies.
Let us all sing Fancy's knell:
I'll begin it – Ding, dong, bell.
        Ding, dong, bell.

Song: *The Merchant of Venice*

1.

A teacher flogs a desk with a pitted rule
a yard long. 'Time!' he is yelling. 'Time!'
An imported beauty from the juniors
squeaks a ball-less 'Where is Fancy Bread'
while we ding-dong under red Shakespeares and gaze
wide-eyed and innocent. Only when the song
has ended, and Beauty has simpered off
to jeers and whistles, and the teacher pounds
bum keys on the jangling upright, preserving
a barrel-organ parody of the tune
as though it meant a lot, do we close in,
baying with ecstasy as his fingers sink
a silent note.
                        We catch him miles away,
force him to wheel, teeth bared, the rule aloft.

2.

That summer. I am lost in unmapped lanes,
lured by music which is England audible
towards an unkempt privet hedge, veined lilac.
And there he sits, jungled in garden, whispering
love-breath to an English flute. His face
is abstract with a young man's softness, all
his fingers, strangely long now, tenderly flutter.
Scarlet runners flaunt extravagant red purses.
Marigolds adore, and spindly cornflowers
bend at him their own weight, like the failure
of all ambition.
I would brood now upon violence,
creep quietly away and brood upon violence,
upon Fancy mutilated in its cradle.
The theme pervasive in the dulcet air.

3.

The game has rules and everyone must lose.
We stand in fidgety ranks and hear him dead.
Some are sniggering. A tired headmaster drawls
the unbearable comedy of his all-round skills:
of helping years of first-years learn to swim,
of coaching soccer teams when he was younger,
much younger. A clamped guffaw explodes.
Last, and minimal, words about his music,
about his life. 'His gift was to engender
a love of music in hundreds of young men
or, where he found a love, to nourish it.'
That night, I dream of Fancy Bread: a loaf
plaited and glazed and starred with sugar stars.
In dream, I gorge it, and awake unfed.

Four Poems

1. *Inheritor*

The man approaching from out the wet trees
in one hand holds a sack, lumpy and with a gloss
of seeping blood in patches, and in the other
an arc of satin sheen, a metal bow.
A quiver of steel bolts nags his hip.
He has been practising the bomb
fallen, perfecting his brainchildren
on rabbits. When that real world comes
his bolts will split people – the marauders,
scavengers, screamers trailing their skin,
diseased children, and the wandering crazed.
He will emerge from shambles as he emerged
from wet trees. He clinks away, stooped
by the blood-bag to a trail that reeks Future.

2. *Aftermath*

A tour of boulevards lined with trees,
stripped trees, and in every tree a body,
hanging, wedged in a fork, pronged by branches.
They are red, blue, mottled like fruits.
It seems that something crassly natural,
a tidal wave, has lumbered twenty feet high
along the streets and hung the bodies up.
For certain they suffered: flayed, handless,
features rubbed-out. But there was no wave.
I cruise these orchards with a band of soldiers.
We are either entering this city
or leaving it. The responsibility
that like a weapon weights my shoulders down
is for work done or still to be undertaken.

3. *Strange Meeting*

This is my place of death. I trail a hand
through water. The skin breaks off and drifts
on the rusty back of the stream. I remember
snow, a pure world and a cold, its trees
thickening with innocent fruit. I pray for snow
as my last memory. But my eyes
wander abroad, mounting through stained stubble
to an ochre sky, then back to a bristling
range of charcoal uprights: trees. The thing
approaching is bandaged head to foot. It carries
animals. Its face is animal-snout, animal-eyes.
It pauses. Looks. Fingers a bow. Walks on.
If I had reached for its animals, it would have killed me.
If it had pitied me, it would have killed me.

4. *Ware Cliffs*

The huge club sandwiches of the extinct.
The species' rainbow-curves, from the first-foot
try-out, through apogee, to darkness,
aeons in tidy widths my fingers span.
I am a cinder, crinkled, screaming, living,
dropping through lift-shaft time, down, down.
I am stored screaming in a nine-inch high
slatted compartment, stretched out screaming.
The centuries in their mountains pile above me.
New oceans, earthquakes, the monumental
rhythms of ice, until a hillside gives
way with a slow slide, and a creature stoops
to loosen the black pattern of my scream,
palming it with pitying incomprehension.

Falklands Veteran

His daughter trails him jealously across the ocean
blue carpet, and claims his knees when he sprawls in soft
chairs. Delighted to be annexed, he luxuriates
like someone in the sunset window of retirement.
The child in bed, he perfunctorily recites a few
anecdotes in the tones of those bleak unbiddable
spirits who have seen truth and no longer give
a damn: French, German, American mercenaries
shot and no questions asked,
Islanders legless on the forces' scotch,
an end to trade, the resignation of the doomed.
So many insights stay local and unbreeding,
except, perhaps, for a special subtle tenderness
in the goodnight kiss of several hundred fathers.

Prospero to Miranda

1.

Once upon a time, I was a tree, the tallest
tree of an island. Let me describe that tree.
I was an uprush, like pressured water,
cresting into dark needles that splintered light.
I was purely beautiful, high as breathlessness.
But I ached, O how I ached with my weight of beauty,
the responsible act of holding the high
head steady against the gaze of admirers,
against wind that breathed a music from me.
My trunk groaned to be so slender, bearing so much.
At night I wept gummy tears and swayed.
And around my shallow roots I felt the sand
and pebbles shiver. I felt treachery.
And beyond, the ominous instability of the sea.

2.

My ache was intolerable. I split and hurled
my pain in a screaming arc across the sky.
It danced and devoured distances. Its gift
was punishing continents for my agony.
It struck, and from its strike huge flowers of flame
bloomed from roots of bone and rubbled brick.
Then it returned and hovered loving near me.
I had made a venom of the light and air.
Sheared to the core with its birth, ugly at last
as I always knew I was, I toppled sighing
and my sigh released us both. I saw it climb
and curve fadingly to the curve of heaven. It became
its own creature. I lay fulfilled. Centuries
rotted me sweet. I settled. I became earth.

3.

This time I dreamed. The dreams were slow and green.
They coated me with shimmer. The roots of dreams
drank from me, and I churned with pleasure. I gave,
I gave, and my giving blossomed and grew
effortless fruits. And there was silence, the silence
of a planet turning through its seasons.
Towards dawn, the dreams grew wild. Spasms fluttered
the leaves of harmony. Rough places surfaced
like eczema, and in one place a cave
cracked blackly open, and from its depths a something
scratched itself and yawned and shambled out.
Its skill was hurting. I felt how it hurt.
It yanked the green. It screamed for a mate to hurt.
It itched to breed. I felt the itch, and moaned.

4.

It crept into my bed and stared at me.
It was a thing of darkness and was mine.
It stretched its face to touch my face and kiss.
I screamed and woke. Again I was that tree,
pure uprush, pure as pressured water,
cresting dark needles and splintered light,
aching with beauty and the need to hold
my head rock-steady like a beacon-flame.
Pray for me on my island. I feel again
unbearable pains, and that thing of light and air
ticking its countdown. I yearn to split and launch.
Cycles of endless grief are promised me.
Pray that I break like a staff whatever pride
it is that hates that creature and sets it free.

5.

Somewhere in that cycle you appear,
wide-eyed and watchful of my face
as the full moon through a window as I sleep,
or the calm ignored meaning of a dream.
I tell you my story endlessly, as a man
imprisoned hopelessly talks to his visitor
across the impenetrable space between them.
I do not believe in you. You exist only
in a myth of innocence on some other island.
And yet you are my daughter, a woman
with her own story, waiting quietly at my feet
in an age-old posture of subservience.
Why do I refuse to speak the words 'Tell me'
like a bucket lowered in a well of sweet water?

Piero's Resurrection

This is Christ Nightmare. One of the soldiers sleeps
gripping a spear-haft with a whitened fist
defining himself against this looming pure
body that weeps blood and glares in triumph.
One thumbs his eyes. One in spread-legged sprawl
freezes from touch of woman to sight of Man,
the tortured Man, the stabbed and broken Man
who buried under stones still comes up staring,
his empty tomb a furrow of bad dreams.
Our Judas here, the one who will awake
to a common hillside and simple dereliction
of duty, is booze-chinned, bestial,
and snoring. He'll take punishment with a shrug
and footslog it with the armies down the years.

Cutting

Straddling his iron seat and earplugged deaf
the man trails a cacophony of whips
and flails the hedgerow, punishing it
to splintered hefts that angle up, war-stakes
for chargers' bellies. Small amputations,
in tatters of cloak-over bark, eddy and bowl.
Endless, it seems, and everywhere the wish
to hurt, and every lane presses a future
like flesh against a blade. It was here,
September and soft, where they strayed,
the husband and wife, blackberrying apart
dreamily, poring over many-globed
fruit in an autumn of assurance.
Now they lash with lawyers and secateur the past.

Her Story

for D.

1.

Long explorations of an eventless country –
from which I awake, backseat in an old car
driven by some invisible. It is all pure Disney,
primary trees more topiary than nature,
a perfunctory sky, and sexless Arcadian children
who tinkle laughter on the edge of a tiny water
then plunge impossibly deep, hoisting on return
armfuls of droplets transforming into jewels.
There could be rain, or the malicious gift of speech,
or the between-legs fruiting poison,
at which I say 'Come home' and obey myself,
back in the car once more and travelling,
the mirror a slab of pool, and that whole world there,
diminished and far away, under a cloud of warning.

2.

Sometimes I stalk, from room to room, the object
of a great hunger, a great thirst,

as tortured as was Heathcliff by his just-elsewhere
Cathy, but without his heroic consolations:
the centre-stage elemental gestures,
the wind-offered voices, the certainty of his right
to disturb even coffins. I can fly to nothing
but kitchen-language: I am hungry, what can I eat?
I am thirsty, what can I drink?
There must be sustenance among this plenitude –
bare water, coloured cocktails, the fruits
of exotic trees and cuisine. I dare not think otherwise.

Sometimes I stalk from room to room, the object
of a great hunger, a great thirst.

3.

A mountain presented itself intentionally,
breast-round and modest, as in a medieval
painting, where men are unseasonably real
in a landscape of ideas, the stones and trees
waiting like doors to be unlocked. Two paths beckoned,
the one refused climbing into approval, the one
chosen burrowing into the mountain's roots.
There, I saw a table with covered dishes.
Every part of me knew it would be satisfied.
But as I sat, a matron faced me across the board
and said 'Come home'. Instead, I found myself
in the next room where a class of women in riot
made pastry-snowballs and pelted one another.
They caught and ate. The classroom echoed laughter.

4.

I lay quite clothed beside a young man on a bed
in this Institution. When he asked to see my breast
I simply bared it. Only when confronted in a room
by the Governor, the Matron and the Young Man
did I try to hide my nakedness. The Governor
confirmed with the Young Man that I was the one
and touched my breast. 'Don't think', he said
moving his hand, 'that I'm not going to touch
down there'. Later, as birdsong brimmed the grey light,
I lay knowing the horror would stick like a burr,
but marvelling at my bravery – to have come so far
so quickly, to risk birth in such a setting, aware
the newborn would emerge to the hands of violators.
I rose naked, and left him sleeping in the bed.

The Room for Women

This is the room for women: plush chairs
with cushions plumped against migraines, warm
lampshades to pause by, reading letters, a carpet
to ease the pacing. It might be a seraglio's
annexe, a bordello's back room where the shared
weapon of ridicule is passed round and sharpened.
It might be the unseen space in every home.
But I know it is the prison for the life-condemned.
Entering, I see you knitting on a settee.
This is the first day. The woman-warder
says to both of us: She will be all right
when she learns to take just one day at a time.
Together we weep as I hear us say:
Don't you think I know that? Don't you think I know?

A First Love

Ignorant of Dante and Beatrice, of
Petrarch and Laura, of all myth,
knowing only the astonishment of adoration,
I trailed her as her slow step grazed
the earth, her pale face lifting sky-pale
god-humorous eyes. A satchel of wind-riffled
pages swung at her shoulder. I yearned
my Keatsian love at her, and dared not speak.
Three years later, a student hauling sacks
for ten pounds a week, I saw her crossing
a grim yard, her hair scarfed back, her hands
careful with papers. I rushed to stand before her,
knowing she would recognise me. She passed
unblinking. Operations had been performed.

A Dream of Healing

When he draws the knife-blade with a feather touch
around his face, it leaves a flow of red,
raised like a welt and glistening, just as
a pen loaded with ink at a graze floods
extravagant shine onto the white page.
He feels no pain. He feels no perverse joy.
It is perfectly natural. Outside
and clamorous against the full-length windows,
the crowd calls to him, brandishing knives,
exhorting him to join them. Instead,
he continues the quiet act, feeling
the skin lift and peel, the rictus
of agreement softening in a warmth of blood,
the enemy, himself, risking a smile.

At Badgers Mount

1.

The images that others have of us
sustain and kill. When I left one gallery
twenty years long and found a flaking
caravan flimsy under tapping apple-boughs,
they paused at the broken gate, the walkers,
and coloured my desolation with their eyes –
a bronzed romantic in his peace-camp,
dropped-out and speculative.
Did he feel substantial, too, and wholesome,
the landowner, to see me picturing him
richly hauling a winter's heat from woods
in silvered lengths? And his wife, brooding
earth-motherly over vegetables in the kitchen?
But for all comes night, and its gallery of mirrors.

2.

Hugging the existence of the last voice
on the emptying wavebands, I survey the dozen
closed companions who had no choice
but to come with me: Edward Thomas, Kilvert, Jefferies,
Wordsworth, Cobbett – a whole consolatory
landscape lugged like a creaking set of some
tatty touring repertory to be assembled
in the teeth of desolation. Doctor Johnson,
for when the mad tide rises. Hopkins, for nights
like this one, now the voice has stopped
and the empty singing starts. No end to the shame
of the cultivated man once the sinking has begun
and his sweating hand reaches to choose among
Arnold, Milton, Shakespeare, Mogadon.

3.

The child lies between two women,
a mother and an aunt. In a distant romantic war
a father muses on the desert sifting
between his fingers, and will soon receive
shrapnel in his bronzed left arm. The white
ship waits to receive and transport him home,
a weight to place in a balance that will never
be redressed. The child stares at one
and then the other. And then into before-dawn
darkness, a world all female, where two vixens
dispute the looming wood, and a moon
hints valleys and secrecies. He unlatches
the plywood door and breathes the musky air.
His feet are bare, but he begins to move
up a long slope steadily, like a drawn sea.

4.

Another caravan awaits him in the wood,
a wreck invaded by waves of nettle and briar,
settling into a past. When the moon catches it
as the boughs stir, it is momentarily
where the princess waits in her cocoon of sleep.
When the moon is hidden, it is awash again
and dingily shipping mosses through bulging
ply. Who stayed here? Did another traveller
punctuate his life one former spring
with dreams and desolations as the apples formed?
And when he left, was this caravan
the husk of a fulfilled purpose, or emblem
of all that a life can expect? Indistinguishable now
from green rampage, except when the moon glances.

5.

Across the walls, the watery dawn-light walls,
blurred spread-hand shadows hurtle – the outside birds
orchestrated to fury by the Spring. They zoom
from hedges where nests have swollen like fruit
to lawns where the worms lie glistening to be cropped.
I ache with the grief of dreams, lie coiled
on a conscious shore with dark waves surging still
from oceans that have toyed and finished with me,
where creatures were faced human, clawed and beaked,
and moaned with pleasure as they ripped and ate –
endless waves of centuries of faces
around whose lips were smiles of stinking blood.
Now brutal, guiltless, the shadow wall-birds leap,
remotely real. I climb a shore towards them.

6.

The starlings are slicks of tar shining poured
on the orchard posts. Their throats crawl iridescence
and throb with song like a heart. Dozens of others
run oil over wet grass. So metaphor should be casual
as colloquialism, and the night-presiding dream
be incorporated into the hand opening the plywood
door onto nettles and the cobwebbed milk-path.
Something infinitely precarious about this hour
hazes over the landowner's clear intentions
among the woodpiles. He is flanked by two children
holding yellow flowers, whose purpose seems to be
a presentation of large watchfulness and acceptance.
A promise of red broods in the apple trees
and everywhere is unhurried recognition.

7. *Approaching Shoreham*

The most intransigent illusion is the good place:
a pair of arms, a cottage by a stream, a lane
to be walked at night towards a lighted window –
if found at last the end to pain and dream.
I think of Palmer's self-portrait, as a blackbird,
oblivious and complete, sings me towards his valley,
how something feminine, suffering, beat at his face
in panic, and fled forever never arriving,
the way on that slope beneath the green of wheat
flee the backs of nervous shoals, flee endlessly.
High on the valley's side come the roadmakers,
a white scar on a green flank. They march
like an army of god, scouring deception. And there
Palmer's moon still rises, the moon he quit to recover.

8. *Newsreel*

This, with all the unarguable blatant caricature
of a nightmare cartoon, declares I am, we are,
the children of war: women hooking dolls onto barbed wire,
butcher-birds aborting the future, and the primed
silos itching to eject their zero spunk.
Between them, the forlorn police have the look
of stunned revelation: nobody loves them,
they are despised most by those who hired them.
They are designed for small-scale beat-up and backstreet
terrors, not apocalypse and symbol.
Somewhere unseen in this mythic confrontation
a woman hangs not a doll but unfinished knitting
begun for me. In the distance, what we breed best –
a row of military awaiting their time to fruit.

Josh

Nothing in this child is abstract or abstracted.
For good luck he gives me a chalk stone painted orange.
Receiving it, I at once receive the smooth
and roundness of good futures. He tells me
I eat woodlice, and places woodlice on his tongue
and swallows. First, he strokes nettles, and afterwards
tells me he strokes nettles and is never stung.
When he sits apart from me among the long grasses
he looks like a nestling egg. The cliff-face abstractions
present themselves unavoidably when I would speak.
The daisy hangs upon the void, like truth in a context,
and words drag the innuendoes of their histories.
Josh's eye admits. His mouth releases. That egg-shape is the clue.
Nothing left over. When he moves, he all moves.

'Merely an impulse to beautify'

Merely an impulse to beautify
finding an enclave of marguerites
sentinels of purpose on waste ground

plucking only at stems and flowers
finding the roots softly disengage
hands filled with responsibility

root stem flower the whole sad story
earthless withering at the wayside
purpose too vast for my purposes

Approaching Islands

Your white Madagascar flowered dress,
gift of a censorious elder sister
bespectacled and hairstyled for efficiency,
swings all its flowers across this hillside,
and your smile of disbelief
lights on me as I climb. Your hands grip
oats and marguerites and purple currant.
You are beginning to arrive. Your hands
will place this small and English haul in a white
vase against the window and then in the tall bed
hold me. I too am learning to arrive.
Midnight. Your arms are tightening on an English
coast of flowers and fruit. My face against you
admits a Madagascar of dangerous blooms.

Talking

Together, as though we had paused in flight
from our own times of danger. You unpack first.
Other people are histories. Ourselves a scatter of snapshots.
Pink the figs burst against the dazzling walls.
The deserted church where you dared God and left disappointed
will crumble no more than then. It is likely that the man
shot in the neck will always be toppling on his knees
towards you, and you a child in a white flowered dress
be the helpless last beautiful thing his eyes see.
Wholeness, perhaps, is the final reserved gift, and he received it.
Meanwhile, in face of our lovers, we unpack the pieces
and yield to tenderness. This feeling of time stopped, or ousted,
or defeated, may be the approximate wholeness we living
are granted, the future glory of our snapshots.

Snowmen

The irony that day, the pure windless one
that always dawns after the night that breeds snow,
to walk perfectly together, hip socketed against hip,
free in love's enclosure, and to witness those gurus
inspecting the world through cinders, their ice-lips
clamped on pipes as though they had reached an unnegotiable
status such as death. All gods are made by innocent
hands and are left dazzling and unapproachable,
crystalline obelisks yearning at the moon.
Successfully, my love, they provoked both relief and guilt.
We had known two people like that, the burnt-out vision,
the agonised dignity beneath inappropriate hats.
And we had known that blinding surrounding emptiness,
that absence of ringing voices, where children had been.

At Lullingstone

Set in an act of Roman will against
the cold North, the dolphins curve their backs
of chipped mosaic, circling the dead hearth –
symbols of fecund joy we gazed at one
sunlit day when we trembled but dared not
touch. Now fingering snow caresses our windscreen
blind and we can barely glimpse the timbers
in whose shelter the remembered dolphins swim.
Your face is brilliant with starlight and distress.
I cull your words with icy fingers but cannot
speak what I hear – a child's whimper, your child's,
as the Romans might have heard beyond the hearth
and haze of imported wine the night-voice
of the dispossessed, suffering, unappeased.

Returnings

Sometimes, all that can be done is to set logs
ablaze in the hearth to welcome you home.
The journey has been so long and baffling, through
forests of talking, consolatory love,
and shared guilts about the faces of children.
This fire is a warm heart, an open hand, generosity,
a third party to do the talking for us.
'It's good' you say 'to listen to music again.'
The pure and floating vowels. The relished r's.
A chanson through a hiss of static years.
'I remember when I first arrived. By chance
I caught French as I scanned on the transistor.
Hearing my language suddenly, I cried.'
The fire speaks. Your eyes glint to its words.

Earth Landing

It is the ordinary that shocks, the ordinary
landscape of my new world. The autumn
gorgeously dishevels the chestnut trees
down there along the lane, and the spired white church
is rooted among those yews with frosted berries
like a rocket content never to take off.
I have taken off, and moved with a rocket's
appalling stillness through Nowhere. Now, it seems
I must come to earth among continuing business –
close-order marguerites bright-eyed and stubborn,
some tissue-poppies, bravery on thin stalks.
I pass a tennis court, wet-black with rattling leaves,
and remember people. They are indoors, waiting
for a friendly visit and firelit reminiscence.

A View

The season's rust ranges along these trees.
The pigeons slam off down the wind, pure weight.
High indolent clouds fatten their gold bellies
and trail the hillsides with nonchalant shade.
My mind is free. Our apple-white and honey
tiny flat was a three-months' crucible.
Your love-flame tested me in glow
and would not let me be until I was.
'Come on. Pain must come out. I can take it.'
There's a violent berry-flower startling the hedge
that I struggle to break for you and bring home
and thoughts I must bring home: my daughter
struggling to breathe and sobbing 'I never guessed.'
I watch the road in the valley travel two ways.

Oxford

We love our children, hate ourselves in them.
Somewhere, perhaps, my son, your secret
iceberg-deep universe that floats daily from me
holds a tiny function to help me forgive myself.
I explode a furious patronising laughter
at your fascist neighbour's door, its tag
odi profanum vulgus et arceo.
You hush me smiling: 'We've found a way
of co-existing. It's mute, precarious.'
This is appeasement, or wisdom. I follow
your gentle figure in Canadian airforce blue
down ancient stairs. I had come to Oxford
to explain parting and the pain of choice.
We have talked exhaustively. Everything but.

The Children of Separation

While waiting for you to come, I imagine you sitting
in a stopped train between stations, feeling
at peace in no-man's-land, where there is no need
to say 'we' or 'our' or 'home', or other impossible words,

where the poppies among the corn
recall distant universal pain
cushioned in history and innocence.
How unusual it must be for you now to enjoy silence,

with no-one to crave your assurance, no-one to grasp
your hands, stare into your face, and guiltily ask
'Are you all right? Are you unhappy? Will you say?'
No-one you must gratify

with tears, or the absence of tears.
Suddenly, you are among the ranks of those
who once seemed as unlikely, as remote,
as the handicapped, the poor, the mad –

the children of separation, those who are given
two Christmases to halve the pain
and find it doubled, those who are more prey
to nostalgia than old men, who have been betrayed

by language and now handle it like bombs,
for whom affection is a thicket of spies, and surnames
amputations with the ache of wholeness.
Every book taken down is inscribed by loving parents,

and albums of photographs refuse to be otherwise.
What can be done with memories?
What remains of the self if everything that was
is now framed in the inverted commas of 'seemed'?

I imagine the brakes sighing to the inevitable,
and the train resuming the purpose of the rails.
Soon you will step out into my story
whose pages for too long I kept closed to you.

We will walk through fields I am still making mine,
and when the time comes for someone to say 'Let's go home'
no-one will say it. On the platform, we will wait to be parted,
your hand clutching a ticket to somewhere rejected.

Globe of Glass

The sunlight lies along these slopes of January
like peace of mind, and steals into the globe
on the green sill. My breath is trembling like hands,
so poised on the edge of becoming otherwise
this lengthening glimpse of unseasonable serene,
so accustomed my breath to cloud, my hands to shift
perfection from its shelf. Worlds as they form themselves
spin emergence from an argument of fragments,
achieving at last a core at rest, around which
what was chaos becomes a dancing slow agreement.
Now, in this sunlight, I can sustain the memory
of you turning this globe in an autumn window
to coax from its bands of colour grainfields with poppies,
airy skies, and clouds like dreaming women.

Cimabue's Crucifix

The galleries are locked now, and the neuter lights
switched off. The prime nudes bleed to a fade,
and still-lifes bruise like apples in a loft.
In our home, real twilight darkens a painted landscape
where a watercolour woman, preserved like a fruit of love,
changes perceptibly. Thought, sadness, years, flood,
will stain from chin to brow the most resistant face
of art. Sometimes, on evenings like this one,
although, supremely ironic, unchastened another
poem struggles to stabilise, the wisest act
seems to be artless enjoyment of the passing
moments. From my palm today, you laughing beside me,
that two-year filly cropped last year's frizzled grass
then swung off, cantered, and lashed the air with joy.

Barbizon

Barbizon, qu'est-ce que c'est?
Enfin, ò est-ce, ce Barbizon?

C'est dans la forêt de Fontainebleau, à l'endroit le plus admirable. On fume des pipes sous les grands chênes, et on peint les rochers de toutes les couleurs. Tu verras comme c'est beau.

1. Prelude

Marguerites in a green glass, the hand that picked
and trophied them still visible in the involved
slow release happening through water.
How did we come not to trust these mundane plenitudes,

expecting always instead the drunkard's
gritty-scalped morning-after poverty,
when the exuberantly joyful is dew to the commonplace
sun, and the full and brimming cup shrinks to a stain

stickily evaporating on a table that must be laid.
Our one true and indiscreet friend is the dream. It reaches
its hand towards us through night's broken window
promising infinite moors and air to breathe, and we preferred

to saw the wrist against the jags of fear, and to awake
reaching for words and the world-voiced morning paper,
pumping sweat for dawn to cool. No-one by nine o'clock
ever received the gift of who we were.

2.

There is a monastic room on stilts, with walls
of ruffled cream, and lilac at the window
swagged like grape but weightless as squirrels' tails.
A stout man on the petite feet of a faun

ghosts a street in springtime nineteen hundred,
celebrating all wondrous unlikely conjunctions
in a tea-brown lingering photograph.
He persists through loss, the way centaur and unicorn

haunt with residue the noonday skull.
He presides over paintings
too full for qualification or aside:
a morning peasant leaning towards his day

with the sure weight of an ear of corn;
a cockerel fat with hue and sheen, packed
at the gorge with voice; a tree
replete against the sky like the world's lung.

Four people arrived here, just as from nowhere
you can be suddenly in a garden at dawn,
the first ever to footprint wet grass,
witness to all birdsung possibilities,

or be in a strange room shackled with smalltalk
finding with a turn of the head
a landscape of distances that shocks a window
and you breathe freely to recognise

the plenitude of the commonplace,
the breadlike availability of the strange.
Our intuitions, in this ten-feet-above-ground gallery,
welcome us to a no longer private view.

3.

We were a small assembly
at picnic under trees planted for fantasy

where aristocrats played yes
to the lives of shepherd and shepherdess

tagging and ragging under the moon
quitting Rameau for a rustic tune.

And one of us sprawled Impressionist
who had lived life clenched as a good man's fist.

And another confessed her plan
to jolt through life in a caravan.

And a third ranged free as air
like a mind released from despair.

And the eyes of the fourth were in dance
to be reclaimed by France.

We reminisced about what we had never been:
painter, rover, unexiled, gipsy queen.

Tree-shadows on the forest-floor.
Sun-shafts like an opened door.

4.

Replete, we push back from the table –
mahogany olive-stones, minarets and spires
of bottles brimming with light, a beach of crumbs –
the joyous debris of a sacked citadel

whose riches still unpack upon our tongues.
We sing. An offering of buried songs –
playground chants before exile,
ballads of white walls and suns,

bawdry of simple marriages, laments
once village-eloquent with fiddles and drums –
astonished to feel not loss but gain,
encamped within our dreams again.

Cargoed with our reclaimed pasts
that needed half a lifetime to discover,
we are ready now to rise, depart.
It is like a song we sing together

this silence, where we each acknowledge
homesickness as the need not to return
but to bring with you. Four roads lead
together out of Barbizon.

5.

Madame will take our photograph! Zut! the customers.
who do they think they are! The carafes in good time
will be replenished, and those yearning jaws,
let them talk achingly of the quiche and ham –

a stretched hunger flowers into a passion
and they will fall upon their food like lovers!
And so she prepares elaborately this ministration.
The tight plump shining forearms, the matron's coiffure,

the organising hauteur – they are all at our service,
dedicated to the perfection of our capture,
as at all times else to the creation of a cuisine
that for ten years has been the glory of this region.

She has recognised a perfect blend of ingredients
in their prime, and drops everything to arrange us,
dispose our smiles and tilt our heads,
peering judiciously at the balanced colours

before a final magician's flourish and a sealing
click! at which we all applaud and she bows.
The camera she hands back is as portentous
as the covered platter she in person brings

to a table de fête, a weeping family reunited,
or an intimate tête à tête where love is disclosed.
And her courteous smile escorts our departure
as a sighing artist releases a masterwork to the gross world.

Return Journey

A summer fog mid-Channel. The slowed
engines thrum like a guitar. Long ago
the French gulls veered and disappeared, and all
but we sank to the reassuring bars.

How your eyes totally receive and give!
Your hair is jewelled and salved in the drenched light.
We are so refugee, so prone
to inhabit this halfway stillness of all oceans

where the quit shore and the approaching are unreal,
invisible and undeserved, and only the yes
of each other's face affirms we move, until fog
lifts, and a breathing ocean frees the bows

and on the skyline a quick scratch of chalk
fidgets in lively atoms: England and home,
words that still hang in vacancy as I mouth them
as the daisy blows at the cliff's edge. The final gift

is to look calmly on the surrounding hills
or walls, on the stretch of moderately
worked garden, the past with its approximations,
the future with its death, and to say

'This is mine' – a daunting task for one,
well past forty, still learning how to say
'This is me'. Now silent watchers join us
as the dancing atoms seriously become

a shore, and green hints of inland
with its roads and loves, towns and disasters,
haunt the amnesiac sky. Whatever we have made
awaits us, to pester us for love

the way you pestered me, a weary walker
emerging from a dark lane to find a moon
blazing where I imagined more dark lane,
and would not let me rest in my preference

for darkness. The place we are flying from
is where we are heading. The dream from which we try
to rise, like a waterbird extended shaking wings,
is where we must settle and call home. The shore

subtly becomes a harbour, then a quay. The light
is crystal and undeceived. Arm linked in arm
we sway across slats, and where the land begins
begins the road, inward, returning, and then on.

After a Move

The garden contemplates itself with puzzlement.
It has forgotten what it is to be a garden.
In whose name will that wall-hung greenery
open buds? What colours will that shrub invent?

Will four people, bearing drinks and bonhomie,
at some time cross that snail-kissed path and fill
the vacancies of those attendant chairs?
Who will they be?

Will there be visitors to memorise the perfumes,
sleep in the summerhouse, and print the grass?
For whom will the blackbird discover scolding?
Who will watch on Sundays from the curtained rooms

the slow hours slide the shadows across the lawn,
and note the bullfinch, and which rose has first
acknowledged autumn with a fallen petal?
Will there be children to leave their playthings strewn

all night in confidence among the flowers?
And when the darkness grows among the stems
and the house is blind and locked as if deserted,
for whose love will the earth receive the showers?

Retakes

What did we expect that made us fearful?
With a camera and a book of photographs
we retraced the old photographer's steps,
stood where he had stood, and gazing through

the viewfinder at faded groups of children
assembled for a long-forgotten harvest
and at men in caps proud by the filled waggons
we expunged them into the present with a click.

Was it the sense of being close to death?
The silences of those brick walls and bridges
before which we pass less felt than rain and sun?
We understood, when opening the pack of prints,

that the fear, the hope, was to find a hint of ghost
grey among the colours of our own time. Nothing.
There was nothing. They had left nothing. But where
they had been, one of each of us, smiling.

Spring Arrival

The scale of things! An eldorado
in a mustard-pot: primrose, celandine, anemone,

lashed in April grass, sensational
on a white shelf against a blue wall,

tiny and perfect, each drumskin petal
flung wide from the golden eyes,

a cram of winking mischievous delight,
pure consciousness unshadowed,

achieved in a rush of two days' sun
after a cold spring breeding nothing,

and this where more than half a lifetime
can with luck arrive, a glimmering small

birth of light spread-armed with welcome
chuckling 'I told you so' in your own home.

My Stick

This is my stick for the long walks,
treacle-brown with a glaring pheasant's head.

It hooks perfectly, lofting into the hills,
it conducts definitive Elgar, it finds the greens,

it chatters a trail through dust to prove I've been,
it drops the enemy where they lurk in thickets,

it fends off ghosts and doubt and disbelief,
it proves the primrose under the dead leaves,

it leans against the stile and stares with me
where the first swallow skims the thickening wheat,

it primes my feet against the hillside slip
and levers me onto the windy top,

it is intolerant of moods
and wide-eyed chops a pathway through the woods.

In Normandy

It seemed we would go unhaunted,
beached in that ark among the woods,
awaking to every last thing we had chosen –
each other, and an unquestioning

elsewhere, absorbed with autumn. The fields
breathed hay, the hot light trembled,
the thickening milk came udder-warm
in dawn superflux from the farm,

the retired baker who had built his dream
solidly upon his occupation
approached us through his goats to bring
chunk bread from his bakehouse basement.

We played badminton among the trees,
mis-hitting shadows,
and at night curious nameless animals
patted the roof and scuffed the walls

harmless and unharmed. And so it seemed,
together on that road at dusk, harvest and orchard
dustily cidrous, invisible cattle-weight
leaning towards us from the faint fields,

until we neared the cemetery, hand-in-hand,
its fretwork of memorial iron
holding against the dark, its glow-worm
photographs, its repeated moons

of porcelain petals, featuring the dim mounds,
and you became at once an anonymous grip,
a consciousness hanging on, your silent scream
prolonging the impossible distance of that lane.

'I hear their voices. They try to claim me.
I am a vessel where they would pour and pour.
I know, when I pass them, what I was born for.
Not death, but for them to live through me.

'Sometimes I think it's worse. Are they my voices
in gene and atom? Are they to be redeemed,
enacted, embodied, repeated endlessly
in my children, my love, our love, in you and me?'

And those were battlefields I crossed next day,
a silence of millions,
and where the small churn hung, pewter-grey,
its dead weight from my fingers,

brimmed with milk from those death-watered pastures,
other lives had gripped, slipped, gone away,
deaths at my hand ready to show their hands.
And I came through woods towards you like a future.

Semur-en-Brionnais

1.

Love is first
enclosure, doors shut,
a minute

inspection of an eye,
a wondering upon
a body being born

or reborn, best at
snowfall, the streets
slowly forgotten,

a growing dumb,
an attentive light
at dawn,

the day inhabited
by magnified birds
and words

inventing themselves.
Its first walk
is dazzled and tottering.

2.

And yet in time it comes
to summer in Semur,
proclaimed in the small Square,

applauded, brought wine,
a cherished omen
like a swallow crossing

a northern coast.
And like that coast it receives
and hosts distances:

those voices in the night,
frog-voice, cricket-voice,
and those eyes of stars

and in daytime the buzzards
mewing like indignant cats
and the svelte lizards

flashing to cracks
brilliant as thoughts
lost on waking

and from that bush
ten kinds of butterfly
all up in a rush

as a car passes
like leaves loosened
by wind in autumn

but settling again
restoring Spring
with their breathing wings.

Love at last
listens, scans horizons,
universal as grass

incorporates whispers,
registers attributes,
is a context for creatures,

is wholly abroad.
It will never be elsewhere
from that pained shocked face

at the opened door
of the village we pass through
never to revisit.

3. *Son et Lumière*

A temperature of events
against the scale of night
the tower blushes, chills, goes gray-dead.
Here are plague-summers, wine-frozen winters,

pipes and drums of a royal marriage,
slippered feet dancing the ruined floors,
a baby's birth-cry floating out
like a white owl from an absent chamber,

slow clack of horses climbing
bearing the messengers of ultimatum,
shock-wave of a revolution.
Then the scattering of stones. Decades now

of nothing, the nothing of life happening.
We sit afterwards with coffee, pernod,
isolated in recognition,
stirring, sipping, intent upon

the unlit stories inside the skull,
while youths wind cables and whisper assignations,
until one risks the top of his old van
to free from wires a paper kite

and return it to the child who flew it there,
not his child, not his village's, nor his nation's.
A slow and generous act, that warms
the roots of speech as it untangles strings.

We leave reluctantly. The road winds,
swinging us round to face what we have left –
a final tricolour of permanent light
outshining moon and stars across the valley.

4.

After the destruction, people vanished.
Outlines imprinted the remaining walls.
All night, we heard moans from the unreachably hurt.
Trees, stopped in full leaf, had no history,

skeleton-pressures on the stone air.
No nostalgia of Spring, no premonition.
On a hillside, looking over a town,
I saw nothing, a meaningless rubble,

and around me the wild marguerites
were stringy remnants from vanished legends.
Only a spattering of poppies
were coherent with an old story.

Two children crouched in the heather, looking at me.
A woman reached for berries at the end of a lane.
At the window of a house, strange mirroring,
a guarded face in horror of the future.

Meaningless snapshots blown from a lost album.
We glimpsed a cat upon the stairs.
A dog's back brushed the bed as we lay there.
In the empty room a baby sobbed.

We fed the fire and lived for its warmth
long evenings, long days. Sometimes the phone
shrilled for help in the unlit hall.
Sometimes we heard gusts of unaccountable laughter

and found that we were laughing.
We ventured walks and on our return
remembered nothing. We handed each other
strange words like stones found in a field –

when, our, once, often, usually.
We held each other like the only things we deserved.
And then, one afternoon, you said 'That horse . . .'
Together we went out and found it there

as we remembered it, a chestnut colt
shining like a nut straight from the shell,
sputtering clods and tracking us
along a hedge to take grass at our hands.

We had begun the making of a past
we might together visit. Now I study
a coin of sunlight spinning on honey stones
beyond our bed, then rise to scrape shutters

wide in an embrace of memory.
The butterflies have returned, random
jigging gracenotes, the trees are breathing,
cows slog their knees through wrenching grass.

And the people will come, as they came last night,
through all the history of Semur, to clap
small unexpected generosities. I look
at my freckled, ageing hands upon the sill.

Their memory returns. Their skills of pain
and possession. Their partial giving. Their proud clench.
They have come with me through their own destructions.
In them rests the morning's innocence.

No Small Murders

There are no small murders. One wound
seeds a landscape and smears cities. History
stares you in the face at every turn. When you ask
what hope is there when people like us fail and fail

the answer is already enacted
on the plains of Europe where Europe manoeuvres.
Fists of dust hang like breath in cold air
behind each one of us. It is how we came.

This destruction will not be removed from the earth
by claiming it was our right, or we did not understand.
The swallow returns to skim the green wheat,
the one promise kept to the children,

and to stare down through water is to find in a tiny
rockpool insignificant against the sea
transparencies with legs and the beginnings of colour,
frail alternatives to absence, eating and spawning,

though the sea might never reach here again and the sun
breed its dryness in a twinkling and all be gone.
The future waits beyond a palisade of ghosts
like the idea of calm water on a wind-ruffled day,

simple, and universal, and easily forgotten,
like the taking of offered hands, or offering hands.